Decodable Takehome Books

Level 1
Core Books 60-118

A Division of The **McGraw·Hill** *Companies*

Columbus, Ohio

www.sra4kids.com

SRA/McGraw-Hill

A Division of The McGraw·Hill Companies

Send all inquiries to:
SRA/McGraw-Hill
8787 Orion Place
Columbus, OH 43240-4027

ISBN 0-07-572306-9
12 13 14 15 16 17 18 19 QPD 06 05 04

Table of Contents

Level I Core Books

About the Decodable Takehome Books

The *SRA Open Court Reading Decodable Books* allow your students to apply their knowledge of phonic elements to read simple, engaging texts. Each story supports instruction in a new phonic element and incorporates elements and words that have been learned earlier.

The students can fold and staple the pages of each *Decodable Takehome Book* to make books of their own to keep and read. We suggest that you keep extra sets of the stories in your classroom for the children to reread.

How to make a Decodable Takehome Book

1. Tear out the pages you need.

2. For 16-page stories, place pages 8 and 9, 6 and 11, 4 and 13, and 2 and 15 faceup.

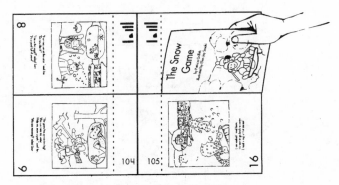

or

2. For 8-page stories, place pages 4 and 5, and pages 2 and 7 faceup.

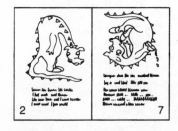

For 16-page book

3. Place the pages on top of each other in this order: pages 8 and 9, pages 6 and 11, pages 4 and 13, and pages 2 and 15.

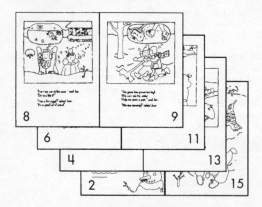

4. Fold along the center line.

5. Check to make sure the pages are in order.

6. Staple the pages along the fold.

For 8-page book

3. Place pages 4 and 5 on top of pages 2 and 7.

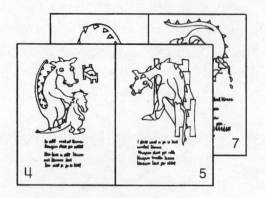

4. Fold along the center line.

5. Check to make sure the pages are in order.

6. Staple the pages along the fold.

Just to let you know...

A message from _____

Help your child discover the joy of independent reading with *SRA Open Court Reading*. From time to time your child will bring home his or her very own *Decodable Takehome Books* to share with you. With your help, these stories can give your child important reading practice and a joyful shared reading experience.

You may want to set aside a few minutes every evening to read these stories together. Here are some suggestions you may find helpful:

- Do not expect your child to read each story perfectly, but concentrate on sharing the book together.
- Participate by doing some of the reading.
- Talk about the stories as you read, give lots of encouragement, and watch as your child becomes more fluent throughout the year!

Learning to read takes lots of practice. Sharing these stories is one way that your child can gain that valuable practice. Encourage your child to keep the *Decodable Takehome Books* in a special place. This collection will make a library of books that your child can read and reread. Take the time to listen to your child read from his or her library. Just a few moments of shared reading each day can give your child the confidence needed to excel in reading.

Children who read every day come to think of reading as a pleasant, natural part of life. One way to inspire your child to read is to show that reading is an important part of your life by letting him or her see you reading books, magazines, newspapers, or any other materials. Another good way to show that you value reading is to share a *Decodable Takehome Book* with your child each day.

Successful reading experiences allow children to be proud of their new-found reading ability. Support your child with interest and enthusiasm about reading. You won't regret it!

SRA Open Court Reading

Lance's Dragon

by Dina McClellan
illustrated by Len Epstein

Core Book 60

SRA

A Division of The McGraw-Hill Companies

Columbus, Ohio

9

Cedric helped Lance and his mom bake apple tarts and bread.
Cedric ate a tart and stopped being bad.

8

www.sra4kids.com

SRA/McGraw-Hill

A Division of The McGraw-Hill Companies

Copyright © 2002 by SRA/McGraw-Hill.

All rights reserved. Except as permitted under the United States Copyright Act, no part of this publication may be reproduced or distributed in any form or by any means, or stored in a database or retrieval system, without prior written permission from the publisher.

Printed in the United States of America.

Send all inquiries to:
SRA/McGraw-Hill
8787 Orion Place
Columbus, OH 43240-4027

Then Cedric felt bad.
"I will give back the scarf and the bracelet," Cedric said.

"Wake up!" yelled Lance's mom. "Cedric the Dragon has taken my bracelet and scarf!"

3

But Lance was brave. He grabbed the lace scarf, and flames licked his face.

6

11

Lance was brave.

"Cedric is a bad dragon," he said.

Lance raced out after Cedric.

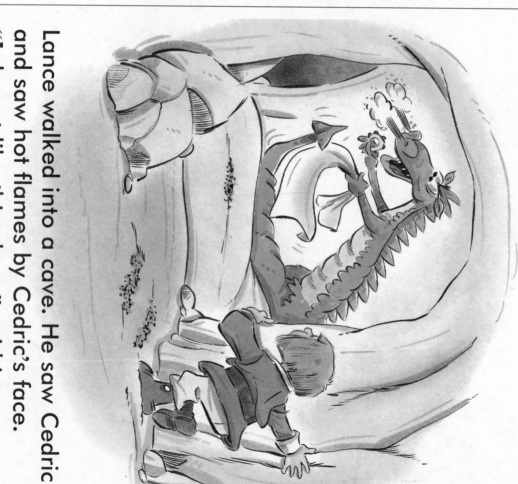

Lance walked into a cave. He saw Cedric and saw hot flames by Cedric's face.

"I do not like this place," said Lance.

SRA Open Court Reading

A Stencil and a Pencil

by Jill Baker
illustrated by Mark Corcoran

Core Book 61

SRA

A Division of The McGraw-Hill Companies

Columbus, Ohio

Cinnamon did not use a pencil with the stencil.

8

13

Cinnamon can use the stencil.

7

14

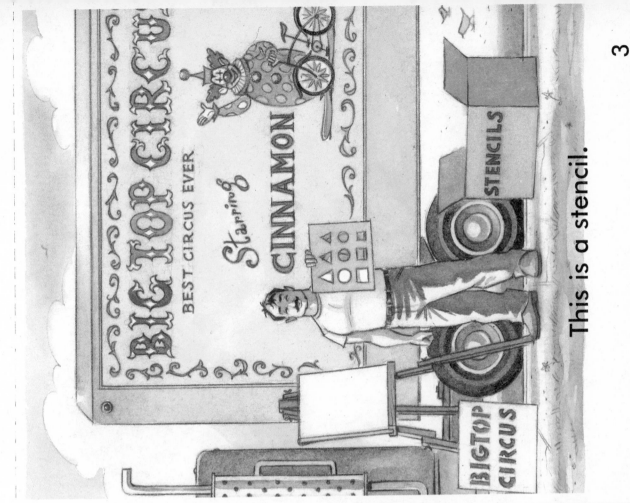

BIG TOP CIRCUS

BEST CIRCUS EVER

Starring CINNAMON

STENCILS

BIGTOP CIRCUS

This is a stencil.

CIRCUS

Tom can use a stencil to make letters.
Tom can use a stencil to print CIRCUS.

Tom can use a pencil with the stencil.
Tom can make shapes.

4

Tom can use a pencil with the stencil.
Tom can make a circle.

5

SRA Open Court Reading

The Pilot

by Ray Elliot
illustrated by Mark Corcoran

Core Book 62

SRA
A Division of The McGraw-Hill Companies
Columbus, Ohio

The pilot can ask Mom for an extra ten cents. "Please, Mom?"

www.sra4kids.com

SRA/McGraw-Hill

A Division of The McGraw-Hill Companies

Printed in the United States of America.

Send all inquiries to:
SRA/McGraw-Hill
8787 Orion Place
Columbus, OH 43240-4027

The plane chugs. The plane grinds.
But then the plane stops.
The plane is silent.
What can the pilot do?

The pilot makes little turns.
The pilot makes bigger turns.
The pilot makes giant turns.
The plane climbs.

6

I put ten cents in the slot.
I am the pilot.

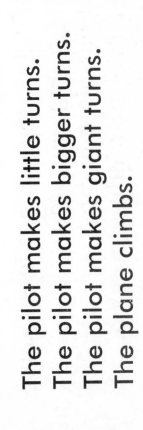

At first, the trip is quiet.
The pilot has fun.

4

But then the trip has little bumps.
It has bigger bumps.
It has giant bumps.
Still the pilot does not mind.

5

SRA Open Court Reading

Spice Cake

by Diane Zaga
illustrated by Deborah Colvin Borgo

Core Book 63

SRA

A Division of The McGraw-Hill Companies

Columbus, Ohio

...and cut a slice for me!

SRA/McGraw-Hill

A Division of The McGraw-Hill Companies

www.sra4kids.com

Copyright © 2002 by SRA/McGraw-Hill.

Printed in the United States of America.

Send all inquiries to:
SRA/McGraw-Hill
8787 Orion Place
Columbus, OH 43240-4027

Stir it a while.
And then bake it...

What is this?
Spice cake?
I can make a nice spice cake, too.

3

Then I'll mix in a slice or two
of a nice ripe apple.

6

I'll add a shake of this, and a little pinch of that.

Next I'll add a plate of diced nuts and nine chopped dates.

Bo and Mo

by Michele Ruman
illustrated by Deborah Colvin Borgo

Core Book 64

A Division of The McGraw-Hill Companies

Columbus, Ohio

Bo is back!
Mo barks and begs.
Bo gets his yo-yo so Mo can
have a snack.
Mo is so much fun.

Bo has left.
Mo takes Bo's yo-yo.
What will Mo do with Bo's yo-yo?
Mo drops Bo's yo-yo into his dish.

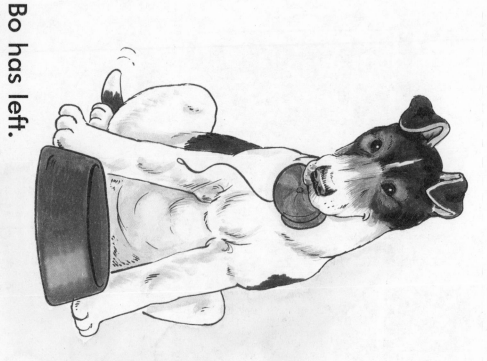

Bo has a yo-yo.
Mo likes the yo-yo.
Bo makes the yo-yo go up and down.
Mo jumps up and down.

3

Mo wants to go with Bo.
Mo barks and begs.
Will Bo take Mo to the pet shop?
Bo tells Mo no.

6

SRA OPEN COURT READING

Bo stops.

Bo wants a snack.

Mo stops.

Mo wants a snack.

Look!

Bo has no snack for Mo.

So. . . . .

Bo will go to the pet shop.

Bo will get Mo a snack.

The Cold Troll

by Amy Goldman Koss
illustrated by Jan Pyk

Core Book 65

SRA

A Division of The McGraw-Hill Companies

Columbus, Ohio

Jake Troll went home and put on his robe.
For once, Jake Troll had no ice on his nose.
"I am not cold!" yelled Jake Troll.
"Thank you, Mole!"

8

www.sra4kids.com

SRA/McGraw-Hill

A Division of The McGraw-Hill Companies

Copyright © 2002 by SRA/McGraw-Hill.

All rights reserved. Except as permitted under the United States Copyright Act, no part of this publication may be reproduced or distributed in any form or by any means, or stored in a database or retrieval system, without prior written permission from the publisher.

Printed in the United States of America.

Send all inquiries to:
SRA/McGraw-Hill
8787 Orion Place
Columbus, OH 43240-4027

2

Mole read Jake Troll's note.
"Do not mope, Troll," Mole scolded.
"Take home this robe."

Jake Troll's old home felt cold.
It was so cold that ice formed on his nose.
It was so cold that his stove froze.

3

HELLO, MOLE.
HELP! I AM SO COLD!
MY STOVE HAS
FROZEN. ICE
IS ON MY NOSE!

JAKE
TROLL

6

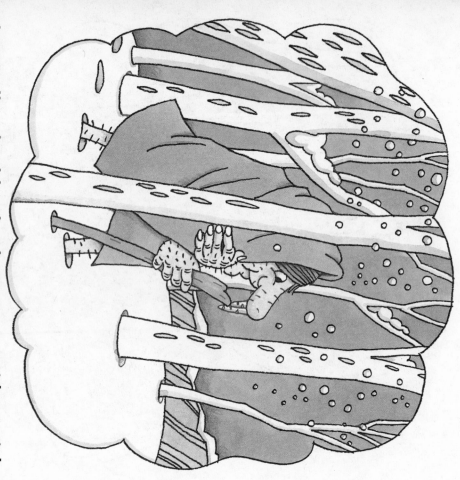

Jake Troll poked his broken stove with a stick.

"This is no joke," Jake Troll said.

"This cold is too much. I have one last hope.

I will go drop a note for Mole."

4

Mole had a nice snug hole.

Cold Jake Troll left a note.

He slipped the note into Mole's hole.

5

Open Court Reading

Rose Takes a Hike

by Rebecca Blankenhorn
illustrated by Meryl Henderson

Core Book 66

A Division of The McGraw-Hill Companies

Columbus, Ohio

Jane makes space for Rose.
Rose thinks a ride is nice
after such a long hike.

16

www.sra4kids.com

SRA/McGraw-Hill

A Division of The McGraw-Hill Companies

Copyright © 2002 by SRA/McGraw-Hill.

All rights reserved. Except as permitted under the United States Copyright Act, no part of this publication may be reproduced or distributed in any form or by any means, or stored in a database or retrieval system, without prior written permission from the publisher.

Printed in the United States of America.

Send all inquiries to:
SRA/McGraw-Hill
8787 Orion Place
Columbus, OH 43240-4027

"Rose is safe!" yells Jane.

"Let's go home."

Mike and Jane like riding bikes
and hiking for exercise.

3

At the lake, Mike finds wet dog prints.
Jane finds Rose under a pile of crates!

14

Jane has a dog. Her name is Rose.
Rose likes hiking with them in the park.

"I will help," says Mike.
Mike and Jane ride for a while.

13

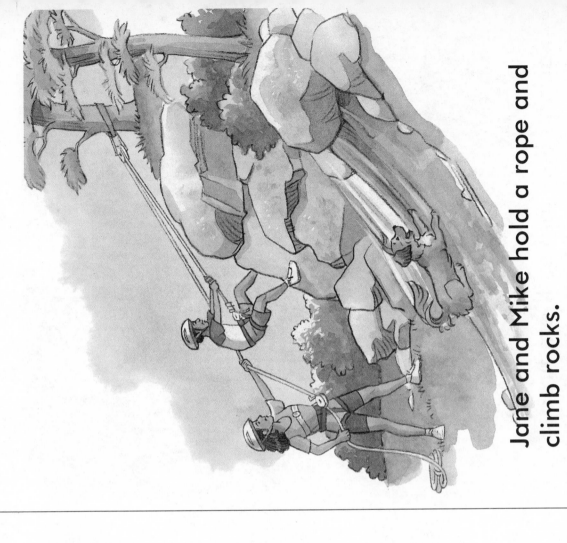

Jane and Mike hold a rope and
climb rocks.
Rose slides off.

5

Later, Mike and Jane wake up.
Jane tells Mike, "Rose is missing!
I hope I am able to find her."

12

Racing bikes makes them tired.
Mike and Jane doze in the shade.

6

Rose hikes more.
Rose is lost, and she whines.

11

38

Rose rolls in a nice place.
She is poking her nose in a hole.

7

Don't go in the cold lake, Rose!
Splash!

10

A spider runs from the hole.
Rose goes after the spider.

8

Rose hikes past some wild mice.
Rose is tasting a pine cone.

9

At the Vet

SRA Open Court Reading

by Linda Taylor
illustrated by Meryl Henderson

Core Book 67

SRA
A Division of The McGraw-Hill Companies
Columbus, Ohio

Val, Velvet, and Vic get in Val's van.
The vet helped Velvet and Vic get better.
Val can have fun with her cats again!

8

2

Val thanks Dr. Kim and says,
"I am glad I came.
Velvet and Vic will get well."

7

43

Val has two pet cats.
Velvet is a black cat.
Vic is a gold cat.

3

Dr. Kim looks at Velvet and Vic.
She states, "The cats ate a bad vine. It
made them sick."
She gives them some big white pills.

6

Velvet and Vic are sick today.
Val must take her cats to a vet.
Val tells her cats, "I will put on a red vest.
Then we will go in the van."

4

They ride in Val's van.
Velvet likes the vet.
Vic does not like the vet.
He hides in the back of Val's van.

5

Music

by Tim Benson
illustrated by Meryl Henderson

Core Book 68

A Division of The McGraw-Hill Companies
Columbus, Ohio

45

Don is a human who makes music.
He makes music with his bugle.

8

www.sra4kids.com

SRA/McGraw-Hill

A Division of The McGraw-Hill Companies

Copyright © 2002 by SRA/McGraw-Hill.

Printed in the United States of America.

Send all inquiries to:
SRA/McGraw-Hill
8787 Orion Place
Columbus, OH 43240-4027

2

Mr. Cupid is starting a new music unit.
It is a unit of new music.

7

Don likes music.
Don's mom also likes music.

3

Don is a pupil in music class.
Don likes music class.

6

Mom says humans can make nice music.
Mom drops Don off for music class.

4

Don plays the bugle.
Don makes music with his bugle.

5

SRA OPEN COURT READING

Muse the Mule

by Dottie Raymer
illustrated by Jan Pyk

Core Book 69

SRA

A Division of The McGraw-Hill Companies

Columbus, Ohio

49

Muse does not like
big branches on his back.
But Muse likes Alfonso's music!

8

2

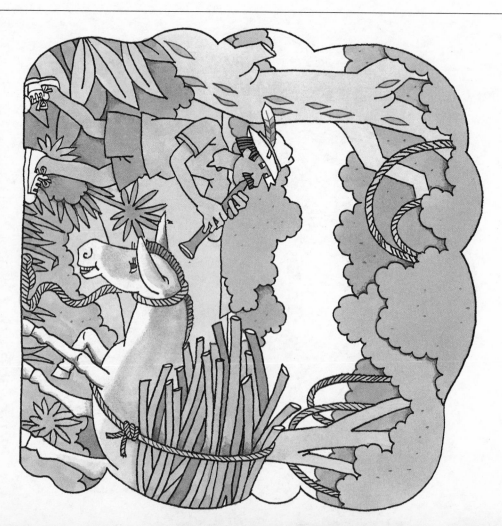

At last Alfonso plays music for Muse.
Alfonso plays nice music.

7

50

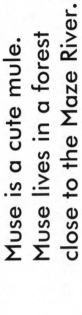

Muse is a cute mule.
Muse lives in a forest
close to the Maze River.

3

Muse does not like branches on his back.
Muse stands still and does not budge.

6

Muse likes the forest and
the Maze River.
But Muse likes music the most.

Alfonso is a trader.
He cuts branches
and trades them at the river.
After Alfonso cuts big branches,
he puts them on Muse's back.

Gem Gets a Bath

by Michele Ruman
illustrated by Meryl Henderson

Core Book 70

SRA

A Division of *The McGraw-Hill Companies*

Columbus, Ohio

Gerald rubs bath gel on Gem with a rag.
Gem is glad to have a bath.
What would Gem do without Gerald?

8

53

Gerald thinks he is finished,
but Gem is still a mess!
What will Gerald do with Gem?
Gerald will give Gem a bath.

Gerald has a large German shepherd named Gem.
Gem is nice and gentle.
Gem likes to run and play.

3

Gerald sees the mess Gem has made.
Gerald must pick up the mess.

6

Gerald tells Gem to run and play.
Gem runs and plays.
Gem also sniffs and digs.

4

Look! Gem has made a mess!

5

Magic Pages

by Anne O'Brien
illustrated by Kersti Frigell

Core Book 71

SRA

A Division of The McGraw-Hill Companies

Columbus, Ohio

57

When the pages end, my magic trip is done.
I am back home in my bed!

8

www.sra4kids.com

SRA/McGraw-Hill

A Division of The McGraw-Hill Companies

Copyright © 2002 by SRA/McGraw-Hill.

Printed in the United States of America.

Send all inquiries to:
SRA/McGraw-Hill
8787 Orion Place
Columbus, OH 43240-4027

I can watch camels run
and giraffes stand in the sun.

When I read magic pages,
I can take a trip.

I can hunt for giant shells
that whisper in my ear.

3

6

I can travel to distant places and hunt for gems.

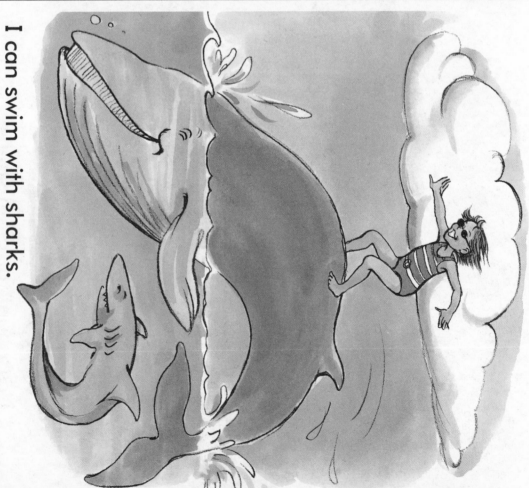

I can swim with sharks.
I can ride on the back of a charging whale.

4

5

SRA Open Court Reading

A Gift for Me

by Jan Roberts
illustrated by Olivia Cole

Core Book 72

SRA

A Division of The McGraw-Hill Companies

Columbus, Ohio

Even Mom likes Sheba.
We all like Sheba a lot.

8

2

Dad likes cats.
He pets Sheba.

7

The cat can be cute.
We like the cat.

3

I tell Sheba my secrets.
Sheba kisses me.

6

Mom and Dad gave me the cat.
It was a recent gift.

4

The cat is female.
She is named Sheba.

5

SRA OPEN COURT READING

Pete and Steve Compete

by Jane Ward
illustrated by Meryl Henderson

Core Book 73

SRA

A Division of The McGraw-Hill Companies

Columbus, Ohio

Pete and Steve are even.
The race is complete.
The race was even.

8

The race is complete.
Who is the winner?
Is it Steve?
Is it Pete?

www.sra4kids.com

SRA/McGraw-Hill

A Division of The McGraw-Hill Companies

Copyright © 2002 by SRA/McGraw-Hill.

Printed in the United States of America.

Send all inquiries to:
SRA/McGraw-Hill
8787 Orion Place
Columbus, OH 43240-4027

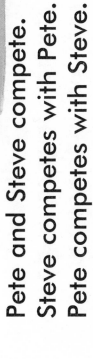

Pete and Steve compete.
Steve competes with Pete.
Pete competes with Steve.

3

Pete is winning.
Steve is winning.
Pete, Steve. Steve, Pete.

6

Here is where they compete.
They compete in the evening.

4

Pete runs fast.
Steve runs fast.

5

Steve Sells Vans

by Dennis Fertig
illustrated by Len Epstein

Core Book 74

A Division of The McGraw-Hill Companies

Columbus, Ohio

I am Steve.
I sell vans.
Can I sell you a van?

16

www.sra4kids.com

SRA/McGraw-Hill

A Division of The McGraw-Hill Companies

Copyright © 2002 by SRA/McGraw-Hill.

All rights reserved. Except as permitted under the United States Copyright Act, no part of this publication may be reproduced or distributed in any form or by any means, or stored in a database or retrieval system, without prior written permission from the publisher.

Printed in the United States of America.

Send all inquiries to:
SRA/McGraw-Hill
8787 Orion Place
Columbus, OH 43240-4027

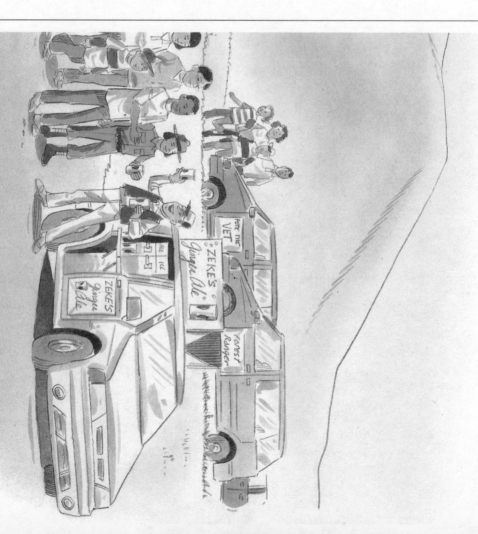

Eve and the five children like the van.
Pete, Zeke, and Val like the music.

70

I am Steve.
I sell vans.

3

Eve can put pages of music in the van.
Eve can put five children in the van.

14

This is Pete.
Pete is a vet.
He likes the huge van.

4

This is Eve.
Eve likes music.
She likes this van.

13

Pete can use the huge van to carry a giant panda.

5

Zeke drives to Gem Cave.
Zeke waves to Ranger Val.

12

Pete can use the huge van to
carry cute pups.
Pete the vet likes the van.

Zeke can drive the van and
sell ginger ale.
The van can make ice cubes.

SRA Open Court Reading

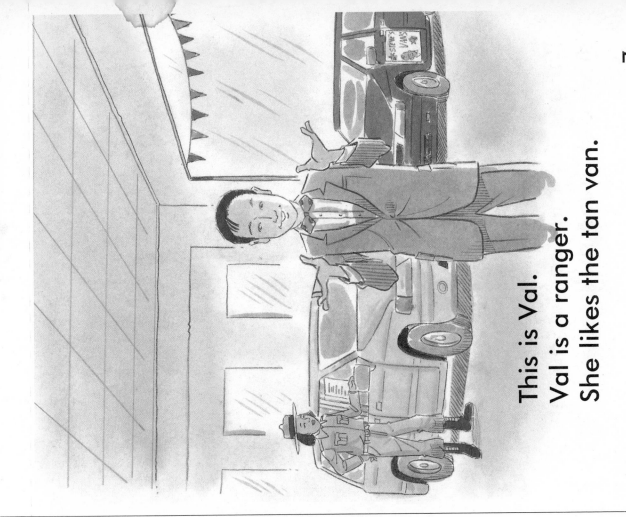

This is Val.
Val is a ranger.
She likes the tan van.

7

This is Zeke.
Zeke sells ginger ale.
He likes this van.

10

Ranger Val can use the tan van to drive over huge rocks.

8

Ranger Val can use the tan van to drive to Gem Cave.

9

The Bee and the Deer

by Mike Sutton

illustrated by Shawn McManus

Core Book 75

A Division of The McGraw-Hill Companies

Columbus, Ohio

77

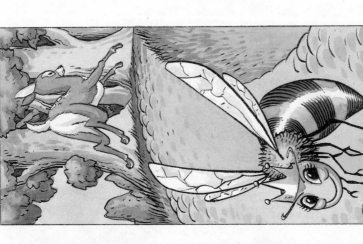

The bee sneezed!
The little deer turned to flee from
the bee back to the green trees.
The queen bee buzzed back
down the street.

www.sra4kids.com

SRA/McGraw-Hill

A Division of The McGraw-Hill Companies

Copyright © 2002 by SRA/McGraw-Hill.

All rights reserved. Except as permitted under the United States Copyright Act, no part of this publication may be reproduced or distributed in any form or by any means, or stored in a database or retrieval system, without prior written permission from the publisher.

Printed in the United States of America.

Send all inquiries to:
SRA/McGraw-Hill
8787 Orion Place
Columbus, OH 43240-4027

The deer did see a bee.
The deer peered at the bee.
The bee peered at the deer.

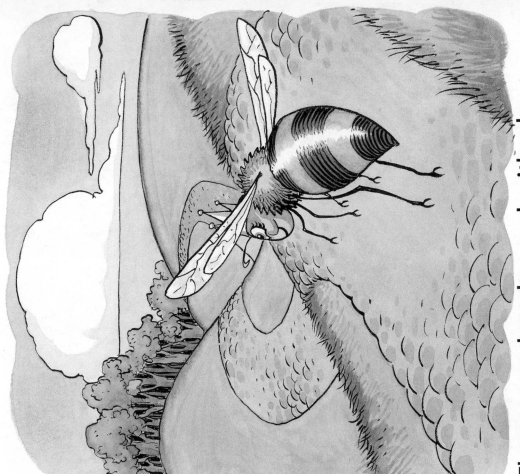

The queen bee buzzed with glee.
The queen bee buzzed down the street.

3

The little deer stopped his feet.
Did he just see a bee?
The little deer felt timid and meek.

6

The little deer left the green trees.
The little deer walked down the street.

4

The queen bee peered down the street.
Was that a deer she was about to meet?

5

80

Dragons Don't Get Colds

SRA OPEN COURT READING

by Dottie Raymer
illustrated by Kersti Frigell

Core Book 76

A Division of The McGraw-Hill Companies

Columbus, Ohio

"Oh! I can breathe!" said Dean.
"My cold is gone!"
"I am glad," Dad said with a smile,
"since dragons don't get colds."

8

www.sra4kids.com

SRA/McGraw-Hill

A Division of *The McGraw-Hill Companies*

Copyright © 2002 by SRA/McGraw-Hill.

All rights reserved. Except as permitted under the United States Copyright Act, no part of this publication may be reproduced or distributed in any form or by any means, or stored in a database or retrieval system, without prior written permission from the publisher.

Printed in the United States of America.

Send all inquiries to:
SRA/McGraw-Hill
8787 Orion Place
Columbus, OH 43240-4027

2

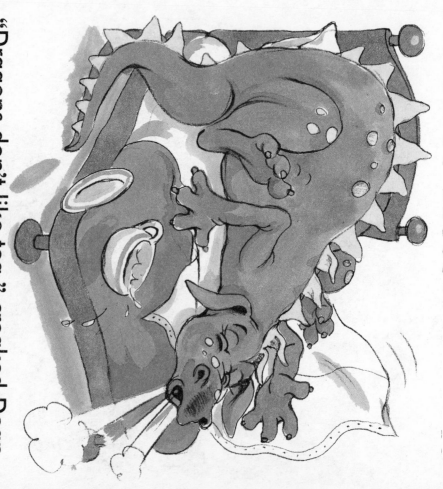

"Dragons don't like tea," creaked Dean.
"Sip it," said Dad. "We will see."
Steam tickled Dean's nose.
"Dragons don't...AH!...get...
AH!...colds!...ACHOOO!"

7

Dean the dragon felt terrible.
"I feel weak," grumbled Dean.
"My nose hurts, and I can't breathe.
I can't speak. I just creak!"

3

"Can you breathe flames?" asked Dad.
"No," creaked Dean.
Dad made a pot of tea.
"This tea's heat will help you breathe,"
he said.

6

83

Dean's dad felt his face.
"Your face feels hot," he said.
"You must have a fever and a cold."

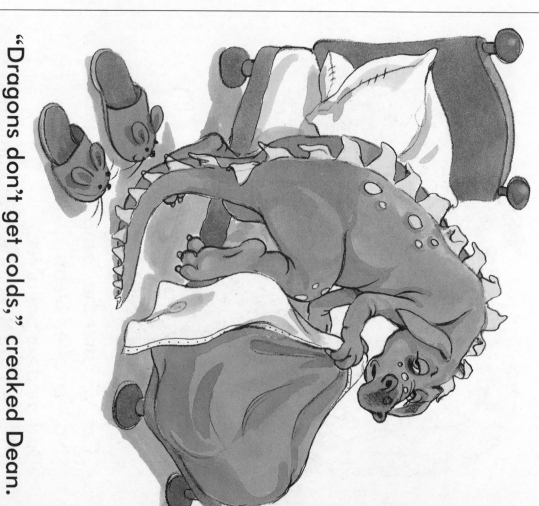

"Dragons don't get colds," creaked Dean.
"Dragons breathe hot flames."

The City Bus

by Sondra Baldwin
illustrated by Olivia Cole

Core Book 77

A Division of The McGraw-Hill Companies

Columbus, Ohio

85

Hurry, hurry!
Catch a city bus.
Where will it take you?

8

www.sra4kids.com

SRA/McGraw-Hill

A Division of The McGraw-Hill Companies

Copyright © 2002 by SRA/McGraw-Hill.

All rights reserved. Except as permitted under the United States Copyright Act, no part of this publication may be reproduced or distributed in any form or by any means, or stored in a database or retrieval system, without prior written permission from the publisher.

Printed in the United States of America.

Send all inquiries to:
SRA/McGraw-Hill
8787 Orion Place
Columbus, OH 43240-4027

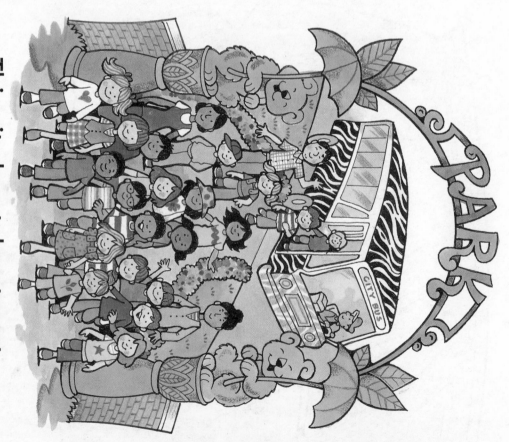

This city bus takes twenty children to a park.

87

Hurry, hurry!
Catch a city bus.

3

A purple city bus takes this
funny man to his job.

6

4

A red city bus takes happy
fans to a game.

A green city bus takes
a puppy to the vet.

5

Nellie and Charlie

by Anne O'Brien
illustrated by Olivia Cole

Core Book 78

SRA

A Division of The McGraw-Hill Companies

Columbus, Ohio

The party is over.
Nellie's babies and teddies are muddy.
The candy is dirty, and the party hats are torn.
Happy puppies lap up melted ice cream.
"Thanks for the help," Charlie tells his puppies.

www.sra4kids.com

SRA/McGraw-Hill

A Division of The *McGraw-Hill* Companies

Send all inquiries to:
SRA/McGraw-Hill
8787 Orion Place
Columbus, OH 43240-4027

Nellie gets out candy and ice cream. Charlie begins to put ice cream on each plate.

"No more help, please!" Nellie tells Charlie's puppies.

Nellie and Charlie like to have parties. They invite Nellie's babies. They invite Nellie's teddies. They invite Charlie's puppies, too.

3

91

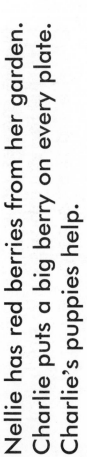

Nellie has red berries from her garden. Charlie puts a big berry on every plate. Charlie's puppies help.

6

Nellie sets up a table in her yard.
Charlie puts napkins and plates
on the table.
Charlie's puppies help.

4

Nellie makes party hats.
Charlie tapes ribbons onto each hat.
Charlie's puppies help.

5

SRA Open Court Reading

Craig Sails

by Alice Cary

illustrated by Kersti Frigell

Core Book 79

SRA

A Division of The McGraw-Hill Companies

Columbus, Ohio

93

"Yes," said Gail. "But for sailing,
you should keep <u>out</u> of the water!
Here comes the rain, Craig.
Grab a pail! It's time for us to bail!"

8

www.sra4kids.com

SRA/McGraw-Hill

A Division of The McGraw-Hill Companies

Send all inquiries to:
SRA/McGraw-Hill
8787 Orion Place
Columbus, OH 43240-4027

"A main? A jib?
I just want to sail, Gail."

"Gail! Gail!
Today I am going to sail!"

"A main?" asked Craig.

"Each sail has a name,"
Gail told Craig. "This little one
is called a jib."

6

"Hi Craig. It looks like it will rain. We should wait and sail later."

4

"Oh, I'm not afraid of rain. We can sail in a little rain!"

"We can sail, but we must be safe," explained Gail. "Wait here, Craig. I'll check the main."

5

SRA
OPEN COURT
READING

No Way

by Jennifer Ball
illustrated by Barry Mullins

Core Book 80

SRA
A Division of The McGraw-Hill Companies
Columbus, Ohio

"No way!" said Ray.
"A tree may not speak in this play."

8

www.sra4kids.com

SRA/McGraw-Hill

A Division of The McGraw-Hill Companies

Copyright © 2002 by SRA/McGraw-Hill.

All rights reserved. Except as permitted under the United States Copyright Act, no part of this publication may be reproduced or distributed in any form or by any means, or stored in a database or retrieval system, without prior written permission from the publisher.

Printed in the United States of America.

Send all inquiries to:
SRA/McGraw-Hill
8787 Orion Place
Columbus, OH 43240-4027

"A tree may not speak in this play," said Ray.

"But a tree has bark," said Kay.

"Maybe you can play a trick," said Kay.
"Maybe you can say, *Bark, bark!*"

6

"I am in this play," said Ray.
"I am a tree."

3

"What do you say in the play?"
asked Kay.

4

"I do not say a thing," said Ray.
"A tree may not speak in this play."

FIRST-GRADE PLAY

SUNDAY, MAY 4

5

The Opossum at Night

by Anne O'Brien

illustrated by Deborah Colvin Borgo

Core Book 81

A Division of The McGraw-Hill Companies

Columbus, Ohio

"It is time for sleep," she tells her babies.
"We might play again tonight."

8

2

The opossum returns to her tree.
Her babies are waiting.

7

The opossum does not like the light.
It is too bright. She sees better at night.

3

Night is over. It begins to get light.

6

When it is night, she wakes.
She hunts for insects to feed her babies.

A dog frightens the opossum.
The opossum freezes. She stays still
and plays dead.
She "plays opossum."

SRA OPEN COURT READING

The King Who Was Late

by Karen Herzoff

illustrated by Anthony Accardo

Core Book 82

SRA

A Division of The McGraw-Hill Companies

Columbus, Ohio

Queen Fay answered: "Dear King Ray is always late. I will save him a piece of dinner."

16

www.sra4kids.com

SRA/McGraw-Hill

A Division of *The McGraw-Hill Companies*

Copyright © 2002 by SRA/McGraw-Hill.

Printed in the United States of America.

Send all inquiries to:
SRA/McGraw-Hill
8787 Orion Place
Columbus, OH 43240-4027

Princess Paige told dear Queen Fay:

"Dear Queen Fay, King Ray may be late to dinner tonight. He does not want you to wait."

The Message

King Ray was late.
"My dear wife might be angry if I make her wait," he said.
"I must tell her that I will be late."

3

Prince Henry told Princess Paige:
"Please tell dear Queen Fay that King Ray may add the right spice and make a fine dinner tonight."

14

So King Ray told his page:
"Please tell dear Queen Fay that
I may be late
for dinner tonight."

4

The maid told Prince Henry:
"Please tell dear Queen Fay that
King Ray might fight thieves in the field
before dinner tonight."

13

109

His page told Sir Dwight:
"Please tell dear Queen Fay that
King Ray may put on a bright leaf
for dinner tonight."

5

12

Sir Dwight told Lord Jay:
"Please tell dear Queen Fay that
King Ray may sail a fancy kite
before dinner tonight."

6

The Answer

Lady Grieves told the maid:
"Please tell dear Queen Fay that
King Ray may invite five greedy mice
to dinner tonight."

11

Lord Jay told the mayor:
"Please tell dear Queen Fay that
King Ray may eat berries on ice
for dinner tonight."

7

10

111

The mayor told Lady Grieves: "Please tell dear Queen Fay that King Ray may heat some really nice rice for dinner tonight."

8

9

SRA Open Court Reading

Why, Bly?

by Dottie Raymer
illustrated by Kersti Frigell

Core Book 83

SRA
A Division of The McGraw-Hill Companies
Columbus, Ohio

"It is hot and dry out here," Bly says.
"I feel better with my head stuck in the sand.
I will stay just the way I am."

8

www.sra4kids.com

SRA/McGraw-Hill

A Division of The McGraw-Hill Companies

Copyright © 2002 by SRA/McGraw-Hill.

Send all inquiries to:
SRA/McGraw-Hill
8787 Orion Place
Columbus, OH 43240-4027

2

"Bly, why do you stick your head in dry sand?" asks a child. "Are you shy?"

"I am not shy," Bly says.

7

115

Bly is an ostrich. She has a small head.
She likes to stick her head in dry sand.
Most animals feel that Bly is an odd bird.

3

"Bly, why do you stick your head
in dry sand?" asks Eagle.
"Why not fly in the sky like me?"

"I can't fly. I am too big," says Bly.
"I like myself just the way I am."

6

"Bly, why do you stick your head
in dry sand?" asks Snake.
"Why not rest in the hot sun like me?"

"I do not like to rest in the hot sun," Bly says.
"I like myself just the way I am."

"Bly, why do you stick your head
in dry sand?" asks Chimp.
"Why not climb a tree like me?"

"I do not want to climb trees," Bly says.
"I like myself just the way I am."

4

5

Dean's Pies

by Jane List
illustrated by Deborah Colvin Borgo

Core Book 84

A Division of The McGraw-Hill Companies

Columbus, Ohio

At the contest Dean tries, but he still dislikes pie.

Dean will not win the contest.

Dean will not even tie the winner.

Dean dislikes pie.

8

www.sra4kids.com

SRA/McGraw-Hill

A Division of The McGraw-Hill Companies

Copyright © 2002 by SRA/McGraw-Hill.

All rights reserved. Except as permitted under the United States Copyright Act, no part of this publication may be reproduced or distributed in any form or by any means, or stored in a database or retrieval system, without prior written permission from the publisher.

Printed in the United States of America.

Send all inquiries to:
SRA/McGraw-Hill
8787 Orion Place
Columbus, OH 43240-4027

On Thursday, Dean wakes up.
He is sick of pie.
Dean dislikes pie.

On Thursday, there will be a
pie-eating contest.
Dean likes pies, lots of pies.
Dean is ready for this contest.

3

Dean still lies in bed.
He dreams of red pies, green pies,
and pink pies.
He dreams of dirt pies and grass
pies and fried pies.

6

Dean lies in bed.
He dreams of pies.
He dreams of apple pies, peach pies,
and cherry pies.

4

Dean still lies in bed.
He dreams of cream pies, custard
pies, and lemon pies.
He dreams of pickle pies, carrot
pies, and bean pies.

5

SRA Open Court Reading

The Farmer and the Doe

by Lisa Trumbauer
illustrated by Meryl Henderson

Core Book 85

SRA

A Division of The McGraw-Hill Companies

Columbus, Ohio

This doe is not a foe!
Farmer Joe drops his hoe.
He cannot be mad at this doe.
He and the doe can both have
tomatoes now.

www.sra4kids.com

SRA/McGraw-Hill

A Division of The McGraw-Hill Companies

Copyright © 2002 by SRA/McGraw-Hill.

All rights reserved. Except as permitted under the United States Copyright Act, no part of this publication may be reproduced or distributed in any form or by any means, or stored in a database or retrieval system, without prior written permission from the publisher.

Printed in the United States of America.

Send all inquiries to:
SRA/McGraw-Hill
8787 Orion Place
Columbus, OH 43240-4027

Farmer Joe stops.
He does not see a doe,
but he sees his tomatoes.
Where is that doe?

He stubs his toe!
That doe brings woe to Farmer Joe.
There goes that doe!
Farmer Joe did not want that doe
to eat his tomatoes!

6

Farmer Joe checks his crops.
They are ripe!
It is time to pick tomatoes!
Farmer Joe gets his hoe.

3

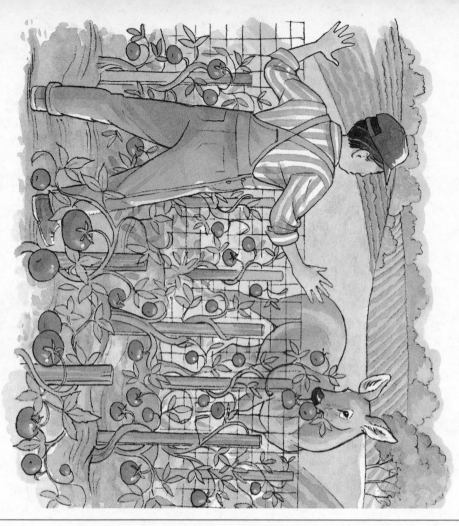

A doe gets his tomatoes first.
The doe likes Farmer Joe's tomatoes.
But Farmer Joe does not like this doe.
This doe is his foe, not his friend.

The doe spots Farmer Joe. Oh, no!
She runs away with some tomatoes!
Farmer Joe runs after her.
He waves his hoe.

SRA Open Court Reading

Load the Boat

by Dennis Fertig
illustrated by Jan Pyk

Core Book 86

SRA
A Division of The McGraw-Hill Companies
Columbus, Ohio

The boat will not float!
The load is too big.

8

www.sra4kids.com

SRA/McGraw-Hill

A Division of The McGraw-Hill Companies

Copyright © 2002 by SRA/McGraw-Hill.

Send all inquiries to:
SRA/McGraw-Hill
8787 Orion Place
Columbus, OH 43240-4027

2

We will load oats on the boat.
Will the boat float?

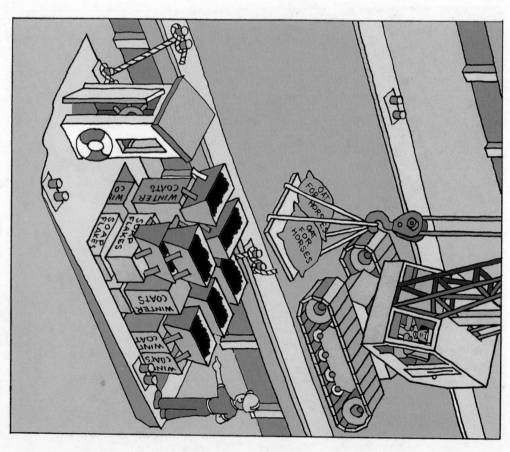

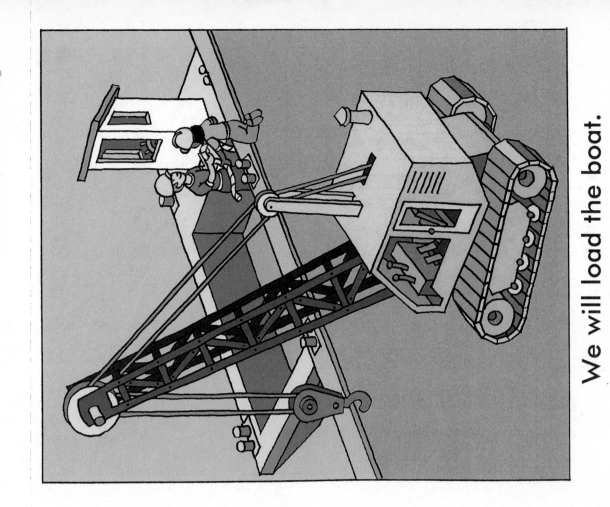

We will load the boat.

3

We will load coal on the boat.
The boat will still float.

6

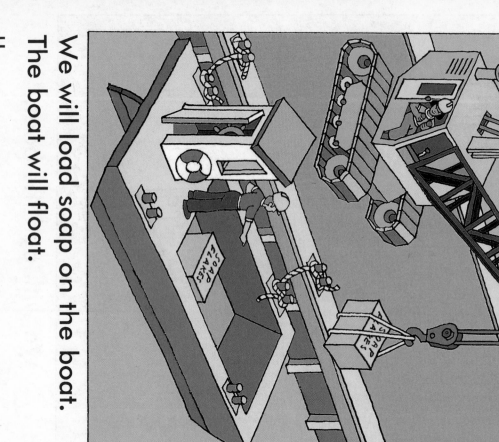

We will load soap on the boat.
The boat will float.

4

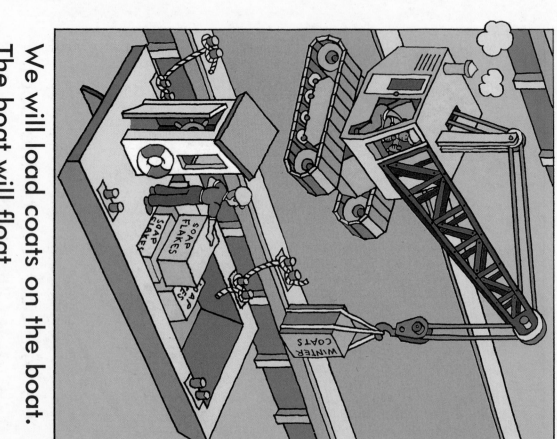

We will load coats on the boat.
The boat will float.

5

Open Court Reading

It Will Not Snow

by Nick Green
illustrated by Len Epstein

Core Book 87

A Division of The McGraw-Hill Companies

Columbus, Ohio

In summer, it will not snow, snow, snow.
We like summer.

8

www.sra4kids.com

SRA/McGraw-Hill

A Division of *The McGraw-Hill Companies*

Copyright © 2002 by SRA/McGraw-Hill.

Printed in the United States of America.

Send all inquiries to:
SRA/McGraw-Hill
8787 Orion Place
Columbus, OH 43240-4027

2

In summer, easy breezes
blow, blow, blow.
Shiny stars glow, glow, glow.

7

We like summer.
In summer, green parks
grow, grow, grow.
Pretty gardens put on a show.

3

In summer, it will not snow.

6

4

In summer, it will not snow.

In summer, little creeks flow, flow, flow.
Happy children row, row, row.

5

Mew, Mew

SRA Open Court Reading

by Dennis Fertig
illustrated by Loretta Lustig

Core Book 88

SRA

A Division of *The McGraw-Hill Companies*

Columbus, Ohio

"Few, few."

2

See? Few kittens are as smart as Mew Mew.

7

My kitten is named Mew Mew.

3

"Mew, mew."

6

Few kittens are as smart as Mew Mew.

4

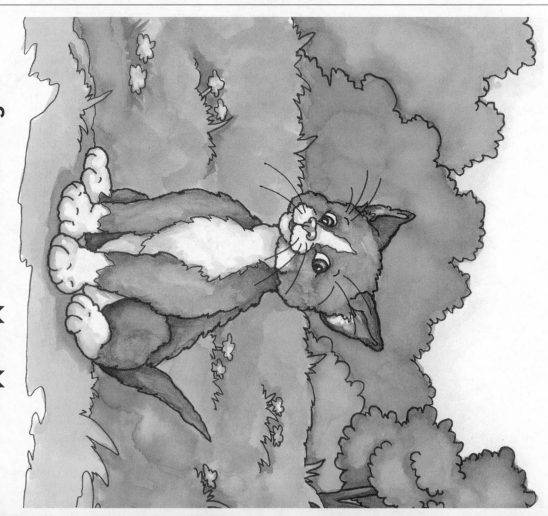

Say your name, Mew Mew.

5

Open Court Reading

Who Will
Rescue the Cat?

by Linda Smith
illustrated by Kersti Frigell

Core Book 89

SRA

A Division of The McGraw-Hill Companies

Columbus, Ohio

Do not argue. We all value the cat.
She will rescue the cat.

8

www.sra4kids.com

SRA/McGraw-Hill

A Division of The McGraw-Hill Companies

Copyright © 2002 by SRA/McGraw-Hill.

Send all inquiries to:
SRA/McGraw-Hill
8787 Orion Place
Columbus, OH 43240-4027

Yes, let's not argue. We all value the cat.
You can rescue the cat.

139

Let's not argue. We all value the cat.
You can rescue the cat.

6

Who will rescue the cat?

3

I will rescue the cat.

No, I will rescue the cat.

I Will Be a Firefighter

by Tim Stewart
illustrated by Kersti Frigell

Core Book 90

A Division of The McGraw-Hill Companies

Columbus, Ohio

When I grow up, I will be a firefighter like my dad.

16

141

www.sra4kids.com

SRA/McGraw-Hill

A Division of *The McGraw-Hill Companies*

Printed in the United States of America.

Send all inquiries to:
SRA/McGraw-Hill
8787 Orion Place
Columbus, OH 43240-4027

Then the dispatcher called.
That was Dad's cue to go.
He and the other firefighters had
to go rescue someone.

My dad is a firefighter.
He goes all over the city and puts
out fires.
Come with me while I visit him.

3

After that, Dad let us try out the truck.
A few firefighters ride in each truck.
Each truck is loaded with hoses and
ladders.

14

Here are the rows of beds where the firefighters lie down and sleep.

Dad had us get down low. That is how to get away from smoke.

Dad and the firefighters eat here.
I sit with them and eat barbecued
chicken and pie.

5

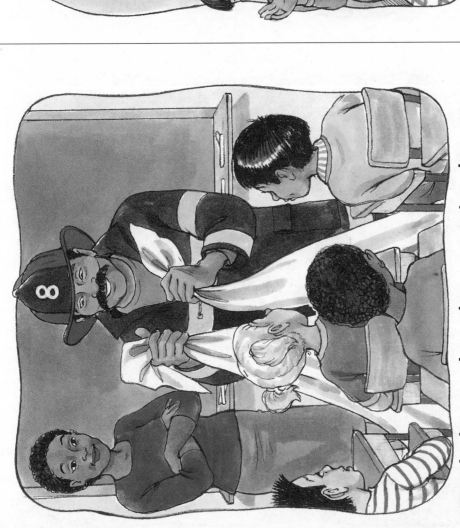

Dad showed us how to tie sheets
together and make a rope.
It is good to have a few different
ways to get out of your home.

12

The firefighters keep the trucks clean.
The hoses are dried and stowed.
One firefighter feeds stray cats.
The cats mew and rub against his legs.

Then we made maps of our homes.
The maps showed doors and windows.

Dad shows me his coat.
The stripes on his coat glow.
The stripes show up in the
smoke and dark.

7

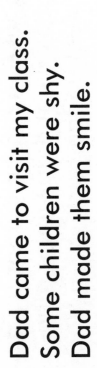

Dad came to visit my class.
Some children were shy.
Dad made them smile.

10

Dad lets me try on his helmet.
He says I will grow into it.

8

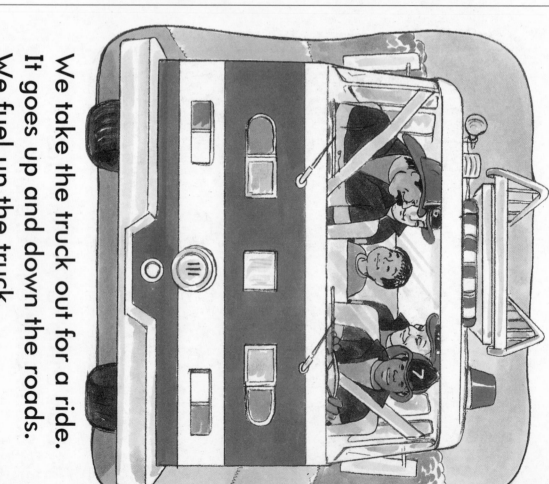

We take the truck out for a ride.
It goes up and down the roads.
We fuel up the truck.

9

Leo the Lion

by Andrew Lunn
illustrated by Deborah Colvin Borgo

Core Book 91

A Division of The McGraw-Hill Companies

Columbus, Ohio

Mom is not fooled.
She sees her spool of thread and the
tools that went BOOM!
"Leo was a lion today," she says.
Then she cleans up the room.

8

www.sra4kids.com

SRA/McGraw-Hill

A Division of The McGraw-Hill Companies

Copyright © 2002 by SRA/McGraw-Hill.

Printed in the United States of America.

Send all inquiries to:
SRA/McGraw-Hill
8787 Orion Place
Columbus, OH 43240-4027

2

Leo the lion gets tired.
His eyelids start to droop.
His goofy mood is gone.

7

When Leo is in a goofy mood, he pretends he is a lion.

3

151

He shoots through Dad's tools. They fall and go BOOM!

6

He zooms around the room.
He hunts a loop of string.

4

He snoops in Mom's thread.
He scoots across her bed.

5

153

OPEN COURT READING

Sue's Clues

by Lisa Rose
illustrated by Olivia Cole

Core Book 92

A Division of *The McGraw-Hill Companies*

Columbus, Ohio

"It is true," said Sue.
"I painted it blue.
It is for you and Mom."

8

www.sra4kids.com

SRA/McGraw-Hill

A Division of The McGraw-Hill Companies

Copyright © 2002 by SRA/McGraw-Hill.

Printed in the United States of America.

Send all inquiries to:
SRA/McGraw-Hill
8787 Orion Place
Columbus, OH 43240-4027

"I see a clue," said Dad.
"You painted it blue."

155

Here is Sue.
Sue is making a gift.

3

"It is true," said Sue.
"I made it with glue."

6

"Hi, Dad," said Sue.
"I made a gift for you and Mom."

"I see a clue," said Dad.
"You made it with glue."

Glue

4

5

157

Flute Music

by Rebecca Blankenhorn
illustrated by Pat Lucas-Morris

Core Book 93

A Division of The McGraw-Hill Companies

Columbus, Ohio

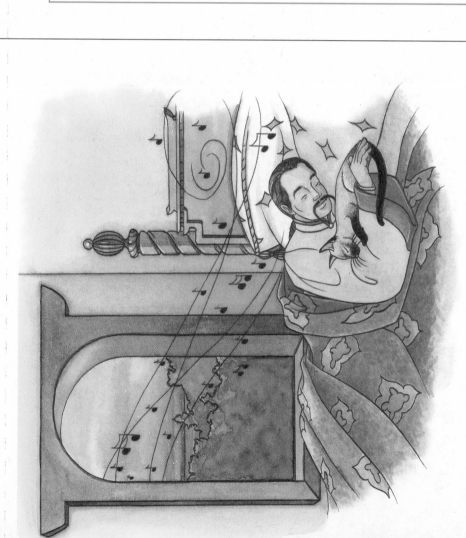

"Yes," says the duke. "Play that nice
tune for me."
The duke smiles at June then goes
home and sleeps to flute music.

8

www.sra4kids.com

SRA/McGraw-Hill

A Division of The McGraw-Hill Companies

Send all inquiries to:
SRA/McGraw-Hill
8787 Orion Place
Columbus, OH 43240-4027

2

Then the duke sees June.

She stops playing the flute.

The duke states, "Who are you?

Your tune woke me up."

June says, "I am June. I did not mean to be rude. May I play a tune to help you sleep?"

7

159

On a quiet night, June plays a tune on her flute. The tune rises like a plume of smoke from a fire.

3

The duke walks in the spruce forest. The tune gets closer and closer. He thinks, "This tune is not bad. This tune is not bad at all."

6

The tune floats past the spruce forest.
The tune goes over sand dunes at the sea.

4

The music from the flute wakes up the duke.
The duke rules in the spruce forest.
He thinks, "How can I sleep with this flute music? This tune must stop."

5

SRA OPEN COURT READING

The TV Crew

by Beth James

illustrated by Meryl Henderson

Core Book 94

SRA

A Division of The McGraw-Hill Companies

Columbus, Ohio

The TV crew used a pump.
That is why the man's arm grew.

8

www.sra4kids.com

SRA/McGraw-Hill

A Division of The McGraw-Hill Companies

Copyright © 2002 by SRA/McGraw-Hill.

Send all inquiries to:
SRA/McGraw-Hill
8787 Orion Place
Columbus, OH 43240-4027

2

On this TV show, the man's arm grew.

163

The TV crew drew clouds
and used thin wires.
That is why the plane flew.

6

On this TV show, the wind blew.

3

The TV crew used big fans.
The fans are big and new.
The fans are why the wind blew.

4

On this TV show, the plane flew.

5

Ruby Tells the Truth

by Ronda Winner
illustrated by Olivia Cole

Core Book 95

A Division of The McGraw-Hill Companies

Columbus, Ohio

I am Ruby.
I tell the truth.

8

www.sra4kids.com

SRA/McGraw-Hill

A Division of The McGraw-Hill Companies

Copyright © 2002 by SRA/McGraw-Hill.

All rights reserved. Except as permitted under the United States Copyright Act, no part of this publication may be reproduced or distributed in any form or by any means, or stored in a database or retrieval system, without prior written permission from the publisher.

Printed in the United States of America.

Send all inquiries to:
SRA/McGraw-Hill
8787 Orion Place
Columbus, OH 43240-4027

It is Thursday.
I have a tuna sandwich.
I am truly sick of tuna sandwiches.

7

166

I am Ruby.
On Sunday, I had a tuna sandwich.
That tuna sandwich was super duper.

3

The next day, I had a tuna sandwich.
That tuna sandwich was all right.

6

The next day, I had a tuna sandwich.
That tuna sandwich was super.

4

The next day, I had a tuna sandwich.
That tuna sandwich was fine.

5

SRA Open Court Reading

Who Took My Book?

by Joyce Mallery

illustrated by Deborah Colvin Borgo

Core Book 96

SRA

A Division of The McGraw-Hill Companies

Columbus, Ohio

Bunny took his joke book and told Bird,

"Thank you for returning my joke book.

I will read it today."

"You are a good friend," Bunny added.

8

www.sra4kids.com

SRA/McGraw-Hill

A Division of The McGraw-Hill Companies

Copyright © 2002 by SRA/McGraw-Hill.

Printed in the United States of America.

Send all inquiries to:
SRA/McGraw-Hill
8787 Orion Place
Columbus, OH 43240-4027

2

"This book makes me laugh.
It is funny!" said Bird.
"This joke book was on the
path home from school.
But I will give it back."

7

Bunny got home from school.
He shook out his backpack.
"Where is my joke book?" he asked.

3

"I heard a laugh.
Should we look here?" Mom asked.
Mom and Bunny looked behind a wood pile.

6

"Oh, no! Where is your joke book?"
asked Mom. "I will help you look for it."

4

Mom and Bunny took a walk.
They hoped to find Bunny's book.
Mom and Bunny looked by the
babbling brook.
No book!

5

OPEN COURT READING

A Clown Comes to Town

by Dina McClellan
illustrated by Len Epstein

Core Book 97

SRA

A Division of The McGraw-Hill Companies

Columbus, Ohio

Chowder tossed flowers to the crowd then said, "The show is over now!"
On the way home Howie said, "Wow, today was a super day. Chowder the Clown came to town instead of rain showers."

8

www.sra4kids.com

SRA/McGraw-Hill

A Division of The McGraw-Hill Companies

Copyright © 2002 by SRA/McGraw-Hill.

Printed in the United States of America.

Send all inquiries to:
SRA/McGraw-Hill
8787 Orion Place
Columbus, OH 43240-4027

Chowder the Clown did magic tricks.
He made a cat bark and made a dog meow.
He changed a fish into an owl.

"Bow-wow"

"MEOW"

174

The Browns stayed inside that day.
It was supposed to rain. Rain
showers would be good for flowers
but not for the Browns.

3

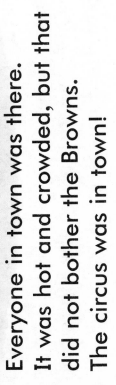

Everyone in town was there.
It was hot and crowded, but that
did not bother the Browns.
The circus was in town!

6

"What are you looking at now?" Howie asked his dad.

"A lady in a gown has a gold crown on her head," said Dad. "Now she is taking a bow."

"Did you know the circus is in town?" asked Howie.

4

"The circus is in town! At the circus there are clowns!" said Howie's dad.

The Browns ran down the stairs and rode the bus into town.

5

SRA OPEN COURT READING

Max the Grouch

by Joyce Mallery
illustrated by Len Epstein

Core Book 98

SRA

A Division of The McGraw-Hill Companies

Columbus, Ohio

Pat went to feed Max.
"Look, Mom!" Pat whispered.
"Max found a friend!"
Max and the mouse were very happy.

8

2

"How about a long walk?" asked Pat.
She and Max walked for an hour.
Now Max was a tired grouch.

7

Pat loved her hound named Max.
But Max was a grouch!

3

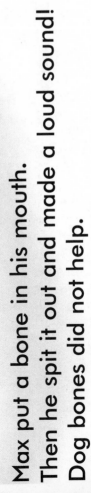

Max put a bone in his mouth.
Then he spit it out and made a loud sound!
Dog bones did not help.
Max was still a grouch.

6

4

"Maybe Max needs a new
doghouse," said Mom.
But Max was still a grouch.

"Does he want a pound of
dog bones?" asked Dad.
Dad put a large bone on the ground.

5

SRA OPEN COURT READING

Our Town Garden

by Rebecca Blankenhorn
illustrated by Susanne DeMarco

Core Book 99

SRA

A Division of The McGraw-Hill Companies

Columbus, Ohio

In winter the garden is frozen.
Flowers are waiting
under the ground.
Next spring, the garden will bloom
and be new again.

16

www.sra4kids.com

SRA/McGraw-Hill

A Division of The McGraw-Hill Companies

Copyright © 2002 by SRA/McGraw-Hill.

All rights reserved. Except as permitted under the United States Copyright Act, no part of this publication may be reproduced or distributed in any form or by any means, or stored in a database or retrieval system, without prior written permission from the publisher.

Printed in the United States of America.

Send all inquiries to:
SRA/McGraw-Hill
8787 Orion Place
Columbus, OH 43240-4027

When fall comes, the leaves fall. The vegetables we took from the garden have all been cooked and eaten. It's time to take the old plants out of the ground. Then we hang bird feeders on hooks.

Planting Time

Our town has a garden that we share.
Our garden is in the town's park.

3

We have a picnic at the town park.
We play tag and shout.
We play until the sun goes down.

14

We plow and rake the ground.
We take out large sticks and stones.
Then we plan the garden.

Our crew works for hours!
Then we are surrounded
by pounds and pounds
of super cucumbers, beans, peas,
and tomatoes.

In spring, flowers bloom.
Around these flowers we plant
seeds that will grow food.
We plant seeds for tomatoes,
beans, cucumbers, and peas.

5

At the end of summer, we harvest
the food that we planted and grew.

12

185

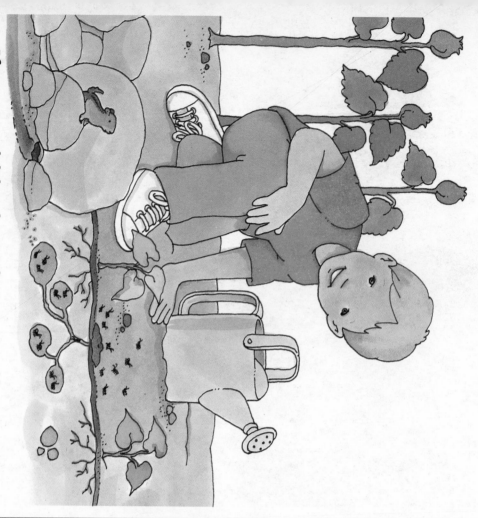

If we could look underground,
we could see how seeds sprout.
Sprouts drink water from the ground.

6

We take good care of the ground
around the plants.
We take out the weeds.
Plants are stronger when they are
not crowded by weeds.

11

Worms and ants dig holes that
make the ground better for the plants.
These holes let air into the ground.

7

Sometimes in June, the clouds get dark.
We hear loud thunder.
Then the garden gets a shower!

10

Sunflowers are gold and brown.
Sunflowers tower over the fence
in summer.
Butterflies and bees swoop around
the garden.

8

The Harvest

Everyone visits the town square
in summer.
Children play all around.
We work in the garden.
But no dogs are allowed!

9

OPEN COURT READING

Paul and the Crab

by Tim Paulson
illustrated by Jan Pyk

Core Book 100

SRA

A Division of The McGraw-Hill Companies

Columbus, Ohio

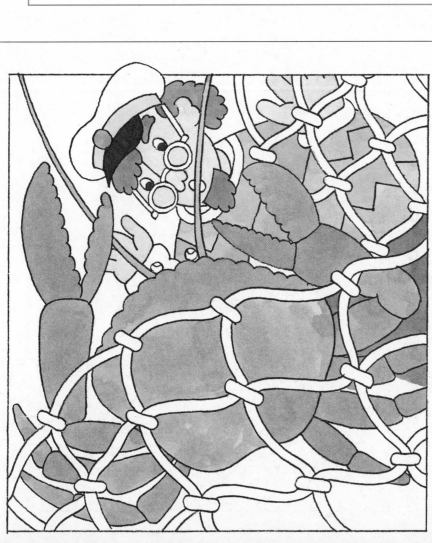

Then Paul hauled in a giant crab!
"My friends Squid and Shark said you
were looking for me," said the giant crab.
"No," said Paul. "I did not mean to haul
you in at all."

8

www.sra4kids.com

SRA/McGraw-Hill

A Division of The McGraw-Hill Companies

Copyright © 2002 by SRA/McGraw-Hill.

Printed in the United States of America.

Send all inquiries to:
SRA/McGraw-Hill
8787 Orion Place
Columbus, OH 43240-4027

"I will haul in a crab if it's the last thing I do," said Paul.
Rain could not stop him. Cold could not stop him. Then finally something in Paul's net caused it to become taut.
Paul pulled and pulled but could not haul it in.

Paul hauled in fish after fish, but he never hauled in a crab.

3

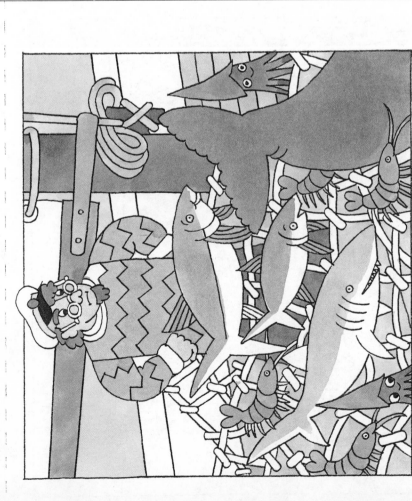

Then once again something in Paul's net caused it to become taut. Paul hauled it up on deck.

"Silly sharks!" said Paul.

"If I do not haul in a crab today, it will be your fault!"

6

"I am going to haul in a crab today,"
said Paul.
Soon something in his net caused it
to become taut.
Paul hauled it up on deck.

4

"Silly squid!" said Paul.
"If I do not haul in a crab today,
it will be your fault!"

5

SRA OPEN COURT READING

Gramps Likes to Draw

by Robert Morris

illustrated by Barry Mullins

Core Book 101

SRA

A Division of The McGraw-Hill Companies

Columbus, Ohio

Dennis paints the shawl blue.

Mom likes what Gramps draws.

Mom likes what Dennis paints.

8

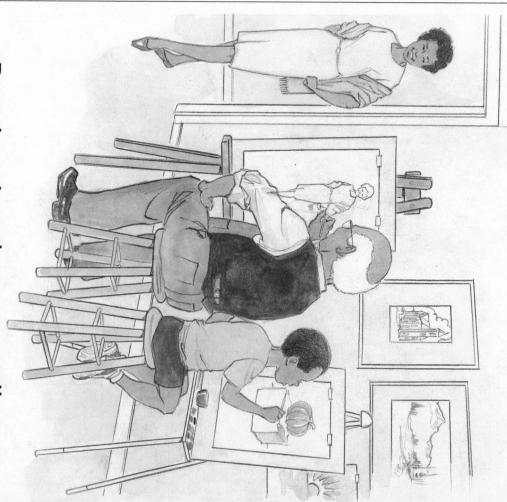

Dennis paints the straw yellow.
Gramps draws Mom in a shawl.

Gramps likes to draw.
Dennis likes to paint.
Gramps draws hawks in the sky.

3

Dennis paints the dawn red.
Gramps draws a pumpkin and straw.

6

Dennis paints the hawks brown.
Gramps draws a home and lawn.

4

Dennis paints the lawn green.
Gramps draws the sun at dawn.

5

196

SRA Open Court Reading

The Knight Who Did Not Know

by Joyce Mallery
illustrated by Len Epstein

Core Book 102

A Division of The McGraw-Hill Companies

Columbus, Ohio

King Knox's knight packed a knapsack.
He left and lived on a farm.
He was happy from that day on.

8

SRA Open Court Reading

www.sra4kids.com
SRA/McGraw-Hill

A Division of The McGraw-Hill Companies

Copyright © 2002 by SRA/McGraw-Hill.

Printed in the United States of America.

Send all inquiries to:
SRA/McGraw-Hill
8787 Orion Place
Columbus, OH 43240-4027

2

His knight got down on his knee.
"I know one thing," he replied.
"I don't want to be a knight any more!"

7

Long ago, King Knox had a knight that
lived with him.
King Knox asked his knight to do
many things.
"Can you tie this knot?" asked King Knox.
"I don't know how," replied his knight.

3

King Knox was getting mad.
He knocked on the knight's door.
"When I ask you to do something,
you say you don't know how. What
do you know?"

6

"Can you sharpen this knife?"
asked King Knox.

"I don't know how," replied his knight,
"but this knife would be good to
butter my roll."

4

"Can you knit some socks for me?"
asked King Knox.

"No, I don't know how," replied his
knight, "but this wool would make
a nice, soft bed."

5

The Choice

by Nancy Morris
illustrated by Len Epstein

Core Book 103

SRA

A Division of The McGraw-Hill Companies

Columbus, Ohio

201

The foil box has a moist cake in it.
The cake has spoiled.
You made the right choice.

8

www.sra4kids.com

SRA/McGraw-Hill

A Division of The McGraw-Hill Companies

Copyright © 2002 by SRA/McGraw-Hill.

All rights reserved. Except as permitted under the United States Copyright Act, no part of this publication may be reproduced or distributed in any form or by any means, or stored in a database or retrieval system, without prior written permission from the publisher.

Printed in the United States of America.

Send all inquiries to:
SRA/McGraw-Hill
8787 Orion Place
Columbus, OH 43240-4027

2

Let's all join in and rejoice.

7

You have a choice.
Which box will you pick?
The box with the coils of silver ribbon?
The box in foil?

3

Nice choice!
You get a box of silver coins!
Rejoice!

6

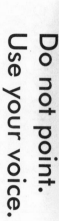

4

Do not point.
Use your voice.

5

The box with the coil of silver ribbon?
Is that your choice?
Don't be disappointed.

SRA OPEN COURT READING

Roy and Big Boy

by Joyce Mallery
illustrated by Jan Pyk

Core Book 104

SRA

A Division of The McGraw-Hill Companies
Columbus, Ohio

"Stop that noise!" yelled Big Boy.
"I want to sleep!"
Big Boy learned his lesson.
He never howled at Roy again.

8

2

Next morning, Rooster woke all the farm animals. Big Boy was still sleeping. All of the animals started howling. Big Boy was annoyed.

Roy was a pig who lived on a big farm.
He enjoyed eating and rolling in mud
all day long.

3

"You are my loyal friends," said Roy.
"You can help me with my plan."

6

But Big Boy the cat loved to annoy
Roy by howling.

4

"Just ignore him," Cow told Roy.
"He annoys everyone."
"We should teach Big Boy a lesson,"
said Dog.

5

SRA
OPEN COURT
READING

Little Wren's Surprise

by Joyce Mallery

illustrated by Deborah Colvin Borgo

Core Book 105

SRA

A Division of The McGraw-Hill Companies

Columbus, Ohio

"We were wrong," said Little Wren.

"It is a tool to fix things."

"You are a smart bird," Dad told Little Wren.

8

2

Little Wren saw a girl come into the yard. "Here's that missing wrench, Ben," she yelled. "Now we can fix my bike."

A wren family lived in a nest in an oak tree. One day they found a strange thing on the ground.

3

"Will it hurt us?" asked Little Wren.

"Let's wrap it up."

But the paper had a big wrinkle. It did not fit.

6

"What could it be?" asked Dad.
He tried wriggling under it, but
it was too big.

4

"Can you write with it?" asked Mom.
Mom rubbed the side with a leaf.
But it didn't make a mark.

5

SRA OPEN COURT READING

Bookworm

by Susan Wong
illustrated by Kersti Frigell

Core Book 106

A Division of The McGraw-Hill Companies

Columbus, Ohio

Trevor will always be a bookworm.

8

2

Trevor wants to be an artist.
He likes to color.

7

Trevor likes to read.
He is a bookworm.

3

Trevor is a narrator in his class play.
His teacher thinks Trevor could be
an actor.

6

Trevor likes to read out loud.
Mom asks Trevor for a favor.

"Don't worry, Mom," says Trevor.
"I will do you the favor. I will read
you the words in the paper."

SRA OPEN COURT READING

Oscar the Bear

by Larry Fletcher
illustrated by Deborah Colvin Borgo

Core Book 107

SRA
A Division of The McGraw-Hill Companies
Columbus, Ohio

He is a dentist.
Oscar the dentist cleans molars.

8

www.sra4kids.com

SRA/McGraw-Hill

A Division of The McGraw-Hill Companies

Copyright © 2002 by SRA/McGraw-Hill.

All rights reserved. Except as permitted under the United States Copyright Act, no part of this publication may be reproduced or distributed in any form or by any means, or stored in a database or retrieval system, without prior written permission from the publisher.

Printed in the United States of America.

Send all inquiries to:
SRA/McGraw-Hill
8787 Orion Place
Columbus, OH 43240-4027

Oscar takes the bus to work.
It costs a dollar to ride the bus.

This is Oscar.
Oscar is a polar bear.

3

Oscar looks at the calendar.
Monday is a work day.

6

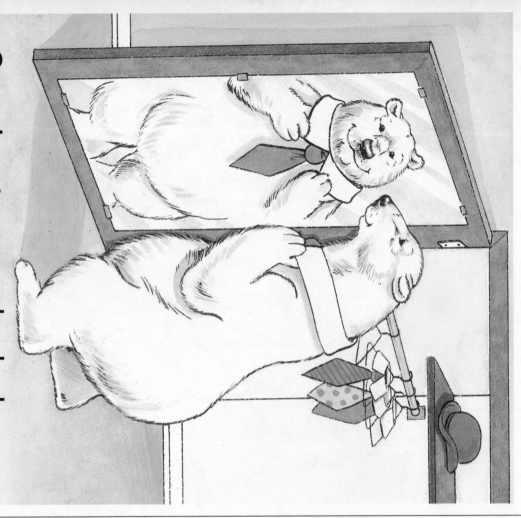

Oscar is not a normal polar bear.
He has a collar.

4

He stays in a nice cellar.
Oscar likes cheddar cheese.

5

SRA Open Court Reading

A Photo for Fred

by Marilee Robin Burton
illustrated by Meryl Henderson

Core Book 108

A Division of The McGraw-Hill Companies

Columbus, Ohio

Phil phoned Fred. "Please come to my place!" he said. "I have a surprise for you! And it barks!"

8

www.sra4kids.com

SRA/McGraw-Hill

A Division of The McGraw-Hill Companies

Copyright © 2002 by SRA/McGraw-Hill.

Printed in the United States of America.

Send all inquiries to:
SRA/McGraw-Hill
8787 Orion Place
Columbus, OH 43240-4027

"Ralph!" grumbled Phil. "No photo for Fred! Ralph will not sit still! A photo is not the best way to see him!"

Phil got a puppy and named him Ralph.
Phil wanted to show Ralph to his friend Fred.
Phil wanted to send Fred a photo of Ralph.

3

"I will take his photo myself!" said Phil.
But Ralph would not sit still.
He barked and wagged and zigged
and zagged.

6

Phil took Ralph to a photo shop. But Ralph would not sit still. He barked and wagged and zigged and zagged.

4

Ralph's photo was a blur. "Ralph!" muttered Phil. "This is a bad photo of Ralph. Ralph looks like a funny pheasant!"

5

The Secret Sauce

by Karen Thacker
illustrated by Kersti Frigell

Core Book 109

A Division of The McGraw-Hill Companies

Columbus, Ohio

The secret sauce was the best sauce Joy had ever had. She took the recipe home and put it in her drawer. Someday she would be a grandma and would pass it on.

16

www.sra4kids.com

SRA/McGraw-Hill

A Division of The McGraw-Hill Companies

Copyright © 2002 by SRA/McGraw-Hill.

Send all inquiries to:
SRA/McGraw-Hill
8787 Orion Place
Columbus, OH 43240-4027

Vapors curled up out of the pot.
The odor was so nice, Joy was sure
the flavor would be nice, too.

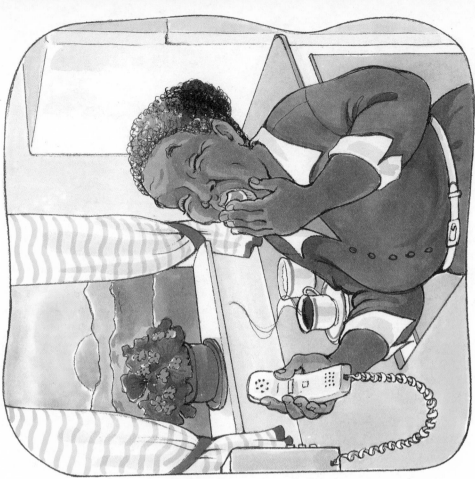

In the morning, Grandma's phone rang. Grandma yawned and answered the phone.

3

"A secret sauce has many secret spices. I will write them all down so you will not forget them. You must protect this recipe like my own mother did."

14

The voice on the phone was Joy's.

"Grandma," said Joy.

"Can I come over today?"

Grandma smiled. She always enjoyed spending time with Joy.

4

"Being a good cook is like being a good person, Joy. You must make good choices. Here is the first choice we must make. How much sugar will we use?"

13

229

"Your voice sounds excited today, Joy,"
Grandma said.
"You can join me in the kitchen today.
We will cook instead of play with toys."

5

"My own mother used to keep her
secret recipes in a vault in the cellar.
The cellar smelled like cedar. My
secret sauce is one of her recipes."

12

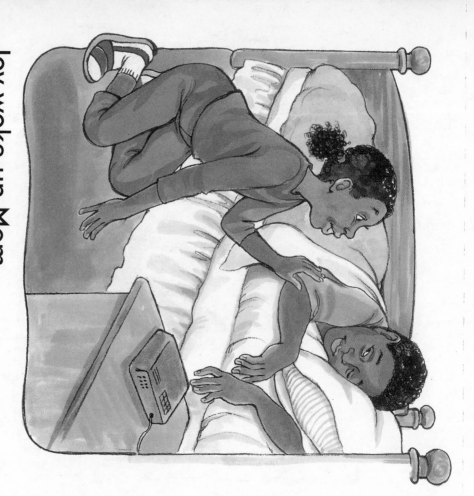

Joy woke up Mom.
"Mom, can you take me to see
Grandma today? Grandma asked
me to join her in the kitchen."

6

Grandma had won a trophy for her
secret sauce.
Grandma opened her box of recipes.
They were in alphabetical order.

11

231

Mom smiled. She always enjoyed
taking Joy to see her grandma.
Mom pointed at the clock.
"I will take you to see Grandma later."

7

Grandma had a shawl.
Her eyes wrinkled when she smiled.
"You are a big girl now, Joy.
I will show you how to make a
secret sauce today."

10

Grandma had plans for Joy.
She took some chicken from her freezer to thaw.
She knew how to make it thaw without letting it spoil.

8

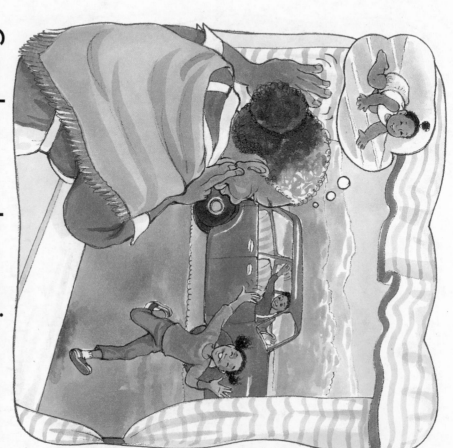

Grandma saw Joy running across her lawn.
It seemed to Grandma that just yesterday Joy was crawling.

9

SRA OPEN COURT READING

The Everybody Club

by Anne O'Brien

illustrated by Gioia Fiammenghi

Core Book 110

A Division of The McGraw-Hill Companies

Columbus, Ohio

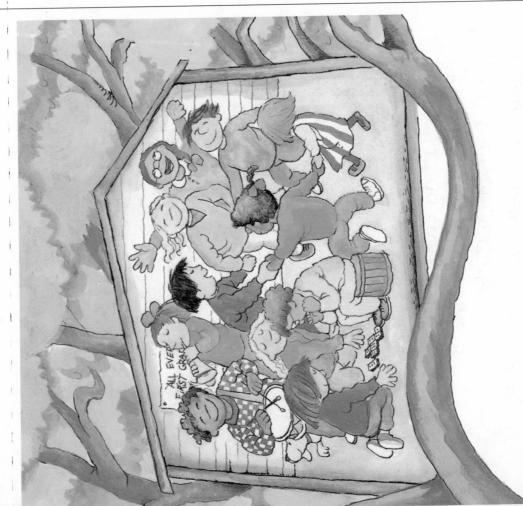

"Welcome to the Everybody Club!"
called Rose.

16

"It's getting crowded!" said Rose.
"How about just calling it the Everybody Club?"
Abby crossed out ALL GRADES and painted EVERYBODY.
Then she painted lots of faces.

The Girls Club

Abby and Rose went over
to Nancy's yard to play.

"Hi!" called Abby's little sister.
"Can I come up?"
"Well," said Abby, "we have a club.
It's called the All Grades Club,
and you aren't even in kindergarten!"

14

235

"Well," said Holly,
"how about the All Grades Club?"
Abby crossed out FIRST,
added an S, and painted ALL.
Then she painted a sixth face.
"Now we are the All Grades Club!"
chuckled Rose.

"Hurry up!" called Nancy.
"We can play in my tree house!"

"Wow! What a neat place!" said Abby.
"Let's make a club!" said Rose.
"We can call it the Three Girls Club."

5

"Hi!" called Nancy's big brother, Tom.
"Can I climb up?"
"Well," said Nancy, "this is the First Grade Club, and you aren't in first grade."
Tom scowled.

12

"Well," said Nancy,
"how about the First Grade Club?"
Abby crossed out GIRLS and painted
FIRST GRADE.
Then she painted a fifth face.
"Now we are the First Grade Club!"
said Rose.

Rose got out paints and paper.
Abby painted THREE GIRLS CLUB
and three faces on the paper.

The Everybody Club

"Hi!" called David. "Can I climb up?"
"Well," said Rose, "this is a club for girls,
and you aren't a girl."
David frowned. He kicked the dirt.

10

"Hi!" called Holly. "Can I climb up?"
Nancy said, "We have a club.
It's called Three Girls Club.
You would make four."
Holly looked down. She hung her head.

7

"Well," said Nancy,
"how about just Girls Club?"
Abby crossed out THREE
and painted a face.
"Now we are the Girls Club!"
shouted Rose.

8

9

241

SRA Open Court Reading

Naughty Max

by Andrew Lunn
illustrated by Olivia Cole

Core Book 111

A Division of The McGraw-Hill Companies

Columbus, Ohio

Max is not as good a daughter as I am.
Max is naughty.

8

www.sra4kids.com

SRA/McGraw-Hill

A Division of The McGraw-Hill Companies

Copyright © 2002 by SRA/McGraw-Hill.

Printed in the United States of America.

Send all inquiries to:
SRA/McGraw-Hill
8787 Orion Place
Columbus, OH 43240-4027

2

"Hi, Mom. Max and I are playing.
Max is my daughter."

7

"Don't be naughty, Max.
Max, don't be naughty."

Mom is Grandma's daughter.
I am Mom's daughter.
I am Grandma's granddaughter.

There is no one smaller than I am but Max.

"Max, you can be my daughter."

4

Max will be a good daughter.

My mom taught me how to make a cake.

I will teach Max how to make a cake.

5

Open Court Reading

Bob Thought

by Andrew Lunn
illustrated by Shawn McManus

Core Book 112

SRA

A Division of The McGraw-Hill Companies

Columbus, Ohio

45

"What if I bought that candy bar?"
Bob thought.
"Mom likes candy bars. I ought to
share it with Mom! Then I know
she'll think I'm grand!"

8

www.sra4kids.com

SRA/McGraw-Hill

A Division of The McGraw-Hill Companies

Send all inquiries to:
SRA/McGraw-Hill
8787 Orion Place
Columbus, OH 43240-4027

"Still, it will take a lot of pennies to get a dog," Bob thought.

"I ought to get something smaller."

Bob thought and thought.
"I ought to save my pennies,"
Bob thought.

3

"I ought to get a dog," Bob thought.
"If I brought home a dog, I bet
Mom would think I'm grand."

6

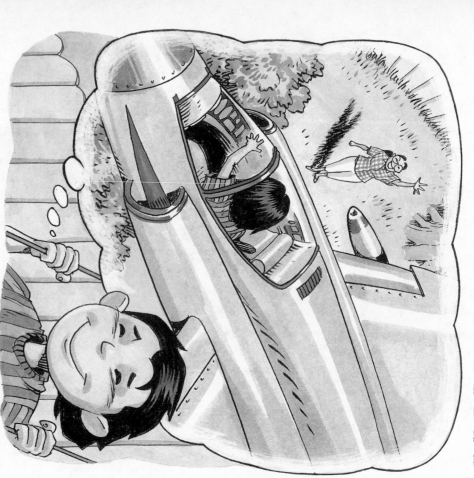

"I ought to save my pennies and get a jet. If I brought home a jet, I bet Mom would think I'm grand."

4

"It will take a long time to save all those pennies," Bob thought. "I ought to get something smaller."

5

24

SRA OPEN COURT READING

Superhero to the Rescue

by Anne O'Brien
illustrated by Meg McLean

Core Book 113

A Division of The McGraw-Hill Companies
Columbus, Ohio

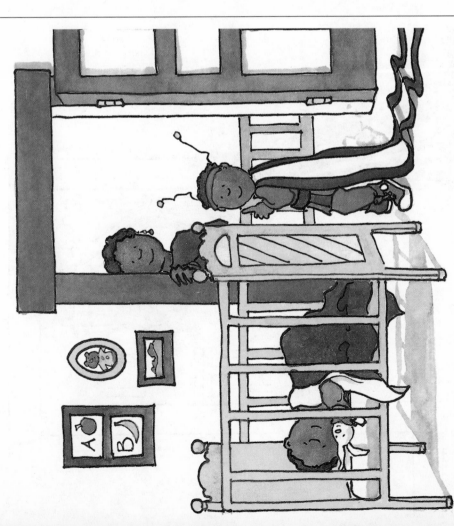

Lenny picked up the bunny.

He put it back in the crib.

The baby stopped crying.

"Superhero to the rescue," Lenny whispered.

16

49

Lenny went upstairs.
The baby was crying.
His bunny had fallen out of his crib.

The Cape

Lenny wanted to be a superhero.

3

At naptime Lenny became bored.
His mom had put Jenny
and the baby down for naps.

14

Lenny put on his cape.
"Superhero to the rescue!"
he shouted.
He raced downstairs.

Lenny's mom found him in the tree.
She helped him get down.
"Play safer," she said.
They went back inside.

13

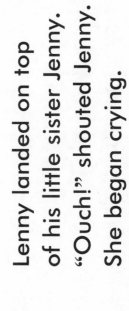

Lenny landed on top
of his little sister Jenny.
"Ouch!" shouted Jenny.
She began crying.

5

"Superhero to the rescue!"
shouted Lenny.
He reached for a branch.

12

53

"Go play quietly,"
Lenny's mom told him.

"Pow! Wow!" shouted Lenny.
He raced to an oak tree.
Lenny's cat sat on one branch.
"Meow!" cried his cat.

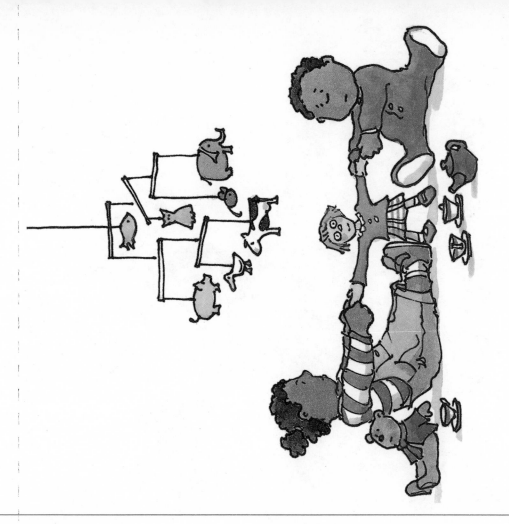

Jenny played house with the baby.
Jenny grabbed the baby's doll.

55

Lenny to the Rescue

"Play something quieter,"
Lenny's mom told him.
Lenny went outside.

"Superhero is here!"
shouted Lenny.
He pushed Jenny out of the way.

Jenny and the baby
both began crying.

SRA OPEN COURT READING

Andy Lee

by Jennifer Jacobson
illustrated by Jon Agee

Core Book 114

SRA

A Division of The McGraw-Hill Companies

Columbus, Ohio

Andy was an artist.
His glass made rainbows dance in rooms.
It also made him brave.

16

www.sra4kids.com

SRA/McGraw-Hill

A Division of The McGraw-Hill Companies

Copyright © 2002 by SRA/McGraw-Hill.

Send all inquiries to:
SRA/McGraw-Hill
8787 Orion Place
Columbus, OH 43240-4027

Andy turned around.

The chair was not knocking and drapes were not swaying.

The tablecloth was not floating.

The hat was not tipping.

It was not dark and scary in there.

Rainbows danced in the room.

Andy Lee the Timid

Andy Lee was a timid man.
He was also an artist and
made stained glass windows.
His glass made rainbows dance in rooms.

3

Andy felt a breeze.
He found a broken window.
He put in the new window.
It fit perfectly.

14

One day, Andy made
a window pane for an inn.
He took the window pane to an
inn that was far away.
Timid Andy walked and walked.

4

Timid Andy walked in.
It was dark and scary.
A chair was knocking,
drapes were swaying,
a tablecloth was floating,
a hat was tipping.

13

26

5

12

Andy came to the town where the inn was.
Down the street ran a maid.
"Turn back!" she cried.
"Do not go!
A chair is knocking.
Drapes are swaying.
It's dark and awful in that inn!"

"Stay with me," whispered timid Andy.
"We will go together."

Andy Lee the Brave

Andy, the maid, and the cook
stood at the front door.
Out ran an innkeeper.
"Turn back!" she cried.
"A chair is knocking.
Drapes are swaying.
A tablecloth is floating,
and a hat is tipping.
It's dark and scary in here!"

"But what about the window?"
asked Andy.
"I am a timid man,
but this is my best window
ever. I will still put in my
window."

10

Andy and the maid came to a gate.
Out ran a cook waving a spoon.
"Turn back!" cried the cook.
"A chair is knocking.
Drapes are swaying.
A tablecloth is floating.
It's dark and scary in here!"

"Stay with me," said timid Andy.
"We will go together."

8

9

SRA OPEN COURT READING

Earnest's Search

by Judy Mills
illustrated by Len Ebert

Core Book 115

A Division of The McGraw-Hill Companies

Columbus, Ohio

It is a pearl!
Earnest did not find gold.
Earnest found a pearl!

8

www.sra4kids.com

SRA/McGraw-Hill

A Division of *The McGraw-Hill Companies*

Copyright © 2002 by SRA/McGraw-Hill.

All rights reserved. Except as permitted under the United States Copyright Act, no part of this publication may be reproduced or distributed in any form or by any means, or stored in a database or retrieval system, without prior written permission from the publisher.

Printed in the United States of America.

Send all inquiries to:
SRA/McGraw-Hill
8787 Orion Place
Columbus, OH 43240-4027

2

He saw a seashell stuck in the earth.
What is that inside?

Earnest liked to swim.
He learned to swim under water.

3

Earnest searched and searched.

6

Earnest searched deep.
He heard there might be gold.

4

He swam along the earth.
Earnest yearned to find something.

5

SRA OPEN COURT READING

The Silly Monkey

by Rose Patterson
illustrated by Kersti Frigell

Core Book 116

SRA

A Division of The McGraw-Hill Companies

Columbus, Ohio

69

The monkey gives Joey the key and
goes back in the cage.
He is a silly monkey!

8

www.sra4kids.com

SRA/McGraw-Hill

A Division of The McGraw-Hill Companies

Copyright © 2002 by SRA/McGraw-Hill.

All rights reserved. Except as permitted under the United States Copyright Act, no part of this publication may be reproduced or distributed in any form or by any means, or stored in a database or retrieval system, without prior written permission from the publisher.

Printed in the United States of America.

Send all inquiries to:
SRA/McGraw-Hill
8787 Orion Place
Columbus, OH 43240-4027

2

The monkey is out!
He rides on the donkey.
He eats the cub's honey.

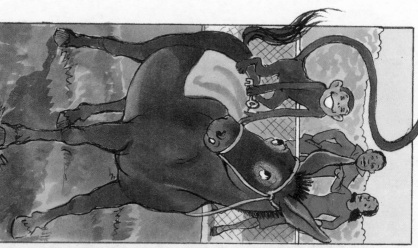

7

27

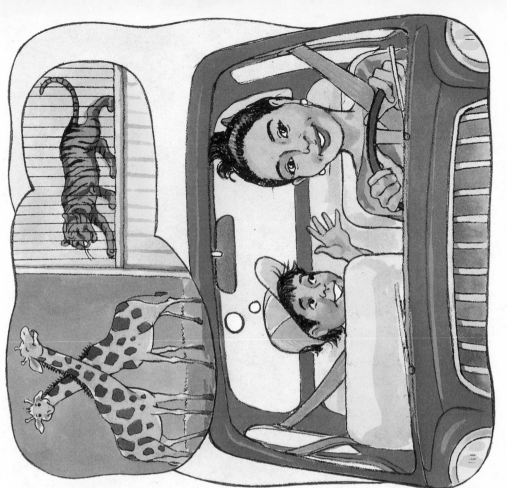

Mom and Joey get in the car.
Joey wants to go to the zoo.

3

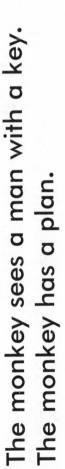

The monkey sees a man with a key.
The monkey has a plan.

6

4

Mom gives Joey money.
Joey rides on the donkey.

Joey sees a monkey.
The monkey makes a face at Joey.

5

SRA Open Court Reading

Tony and Dom Go West

by Lisa Rose

illustrated by Kersti Frigell

Core Book 117

SRA

A Division of The McGraw-Hill Companies

Columbus, Ohio

Tony wins the competition!
His prize is one million dollars.
What a fun vacation!

8

www.sra4kids.com

SRA/McGraw-Hill

A Division of The McGraw-Hill Companies

Copyright © 2002 by SRA/McGraw-Hill.

All rights reserved. Except as permitted under the United States Copyright Act, no part of this publication may be reproduced or distributed in any form or by any means, or stored in a database or retrieval system, without prior written permission from the publisher.

Printed in the United States of America.

Send all inquiries to:
SRA/McGraw-Hill
8787 Orion Place
Columbus, OH 43240-4027

2

Tony rides the stallion.
Dom pays close attention.

7

27

Tony and Dom want to go
on a vacation.

3

Tony and Dom are ready for action.
Tony enters a competition.

6

Tony and Dom go to the train station. The vacation will be a trip across the nation!

4

The train leaves the station. It heads west across the nation.

5

OPEN COURT READING

How the Rabbit Caught the Tiger

by Patricia Griffith
illustrated by Pat Doyle

Core Book 118

SRA
A Division of The McGraw-Hill Companies

Columbus, Ohio

Rabbit giggled and scampered away.
He had tricked a mighty tiger!

16

2

Tiger pulled and pulled,
but his tail did not come out.
It was frozen in solid ice!

"I'm going to get you, Rabbit!"
roared Tiger.
But he could not budge at all.

15

27

The Rabbit and the Tiger

One winter's eve,
a mighty and hungry tiger
trapped a tiny rabbit.

3

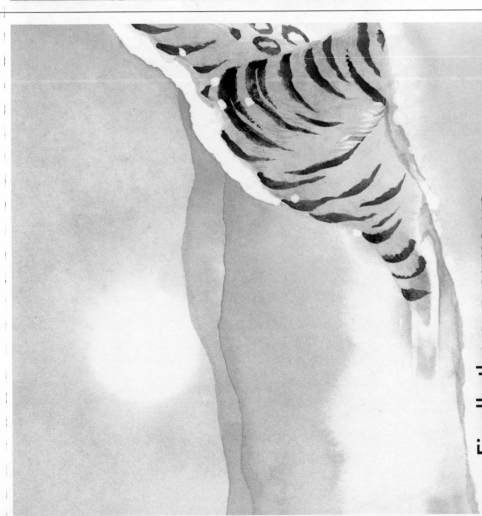

Finally the sun came up.
Tiger's tail felt quite heavy.
"It is time!" called Tiger.
"I am pulling my fish out now!"

14

"Do not eat me!" cried Rabbit.
"I am too small to make a good meal.
If you let me go, I will show you
how to catch all the fish you can eat."

4

The greedy tiger waited longer.
It grew colder and colder.
His tail grew heavier.

13

28

Tiger was greedy.
His hunger was bigger than his brain.
"Show me now, or I will eat you, Rabbit!"
he roared.
Then he let Rabbit go.

5

"Oh, no!" cried Rabbit.
"If you wait until morning,
you will have more fish to eat!"

12

Rabbit led Tiger down to a river.
Rabbit told Tiger, "Put your tail in
the water."

6

11

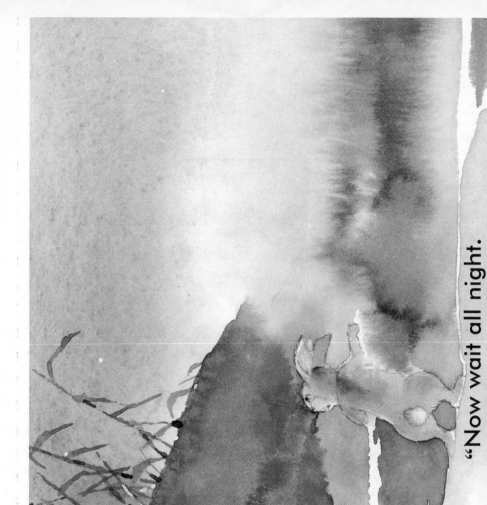

"Now wait all night.
Fish will grab onto your tail.
Soon your tail will grow heavy.
Then you can pull it out
and eat all the fish!"

The Rabbit's Trick

"Is your tail getting heavy?"
called Rabbit.

"Oh yes!" replied Tiger.
"I must be catching lots of fish!
Should I pull my tail out now?"

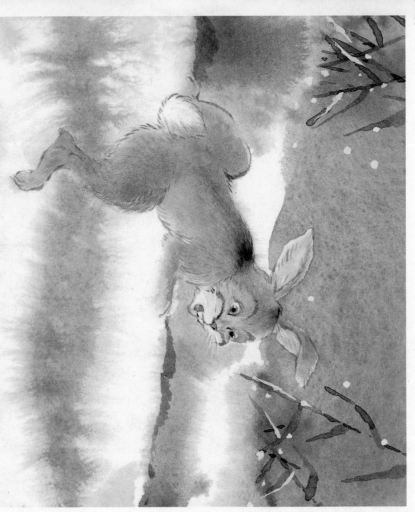

"I'll stay close by," whispered Rabbit.
"I will let you know when
you have caught plenty of fish."
Rabbit climbed up the riverbank,
sat down, and watched Tiger.

8

Tiger put his tail into the river.
He waited and waited.
It grew cold and dark.

9